Noemí Fabra

Translated by Gabriella Aldeman

THE

HEART

HISTORY, SCIENCE
AND LOTS OF LOVE

post wave

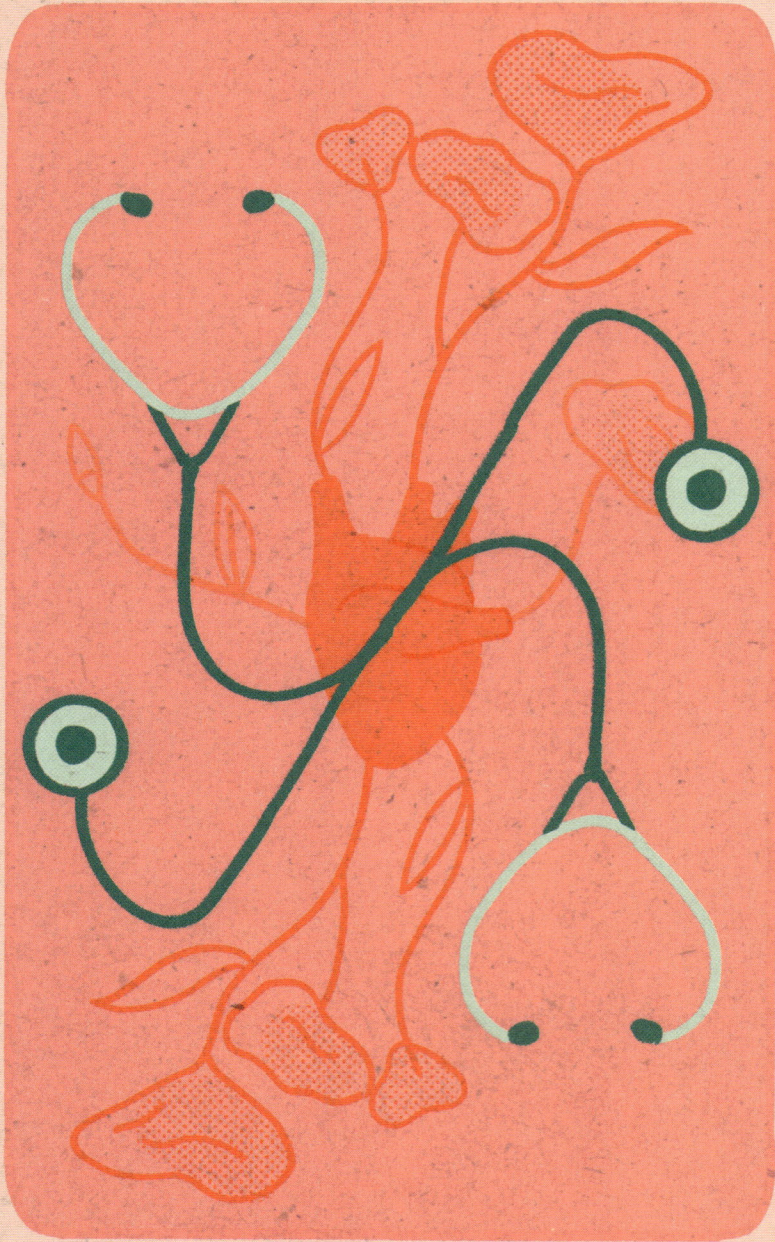

THE SCIENCE OF THE HEART

The heart sits just left of the middle of the chest. It is the epicentre of the circulatory system and plays a vital role in pumping blood around the body. The heart beats more than 100,000 times a day. It is the first organ to form while a baby is growing in the womb.

THE FIRST ORGAN

Growing a Tiny Heart

The first signs of a baby's heart appear as a tiny tube that starts pulsing at around week five or six of pregnancy.

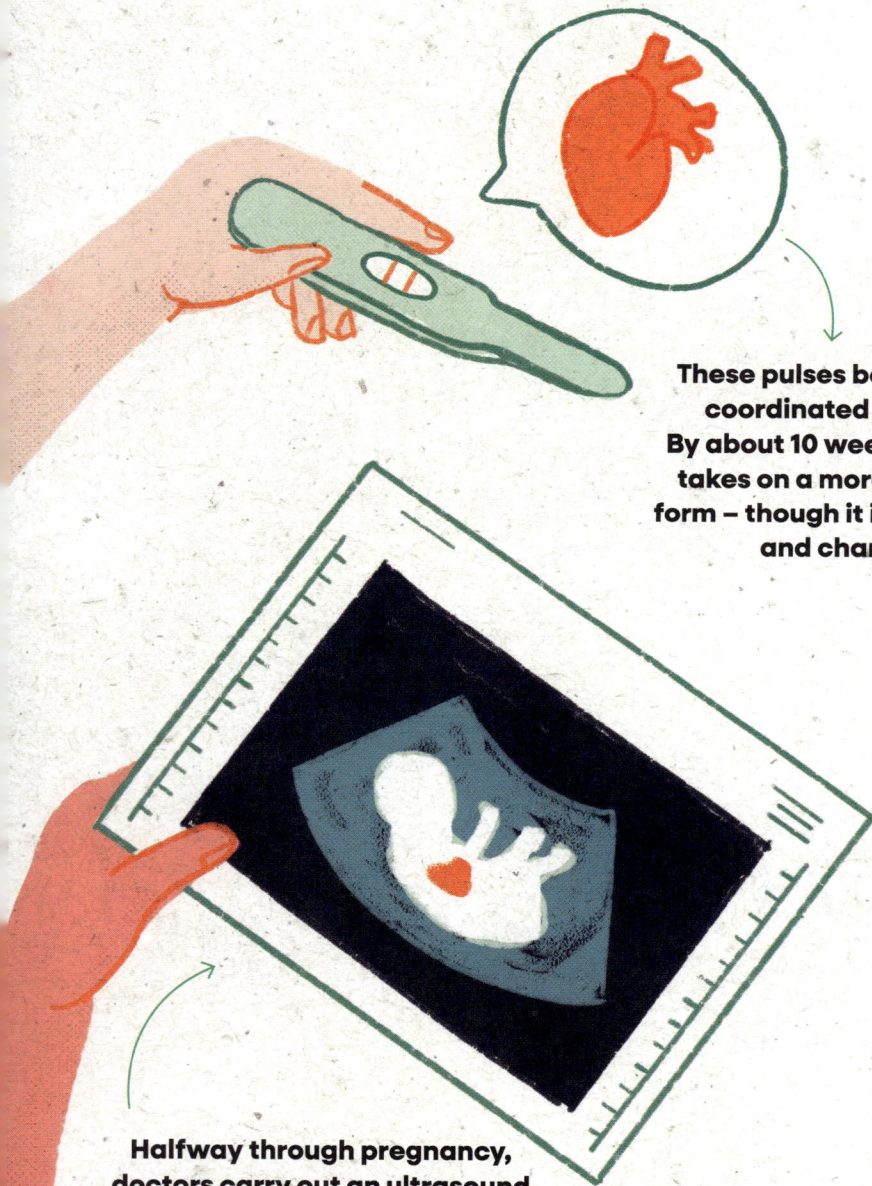

These pulses become more coordinated over time. By about 10 weeks, the heart takes on a more developed form – though it is still growing and changing.

Halfway through pregnancy, doctors carry out an ultrasound scan of the mother's womb to check that the baby is healthy and their heart is growing strong.

18 days

20 days

21 days

22 days

23 days

24 days

35 days

A baby's heart sounds like a galloping horse!

Mum's Amazing Heart

During pregnancy, the left ventricle (one of the four chambers of the heart) gets bigger to pump extra blood. It can increase by up to 50%! This extra blood flow helps deliver oxygen and nutrients the baby needs to grow and develop.

HOW BIG IS THE HEART?

The human heart is located in the chest. It sits between the lungs, behind the breastbone and in front of the spine. It sits inside a special sac called the 'pericardium', which has two layers. These layers hold a fluid that protects the heart and helps reduce friction as it beats.

A person's heart is about the same size as their closed fist. In adults, this is around 12.5cm long.

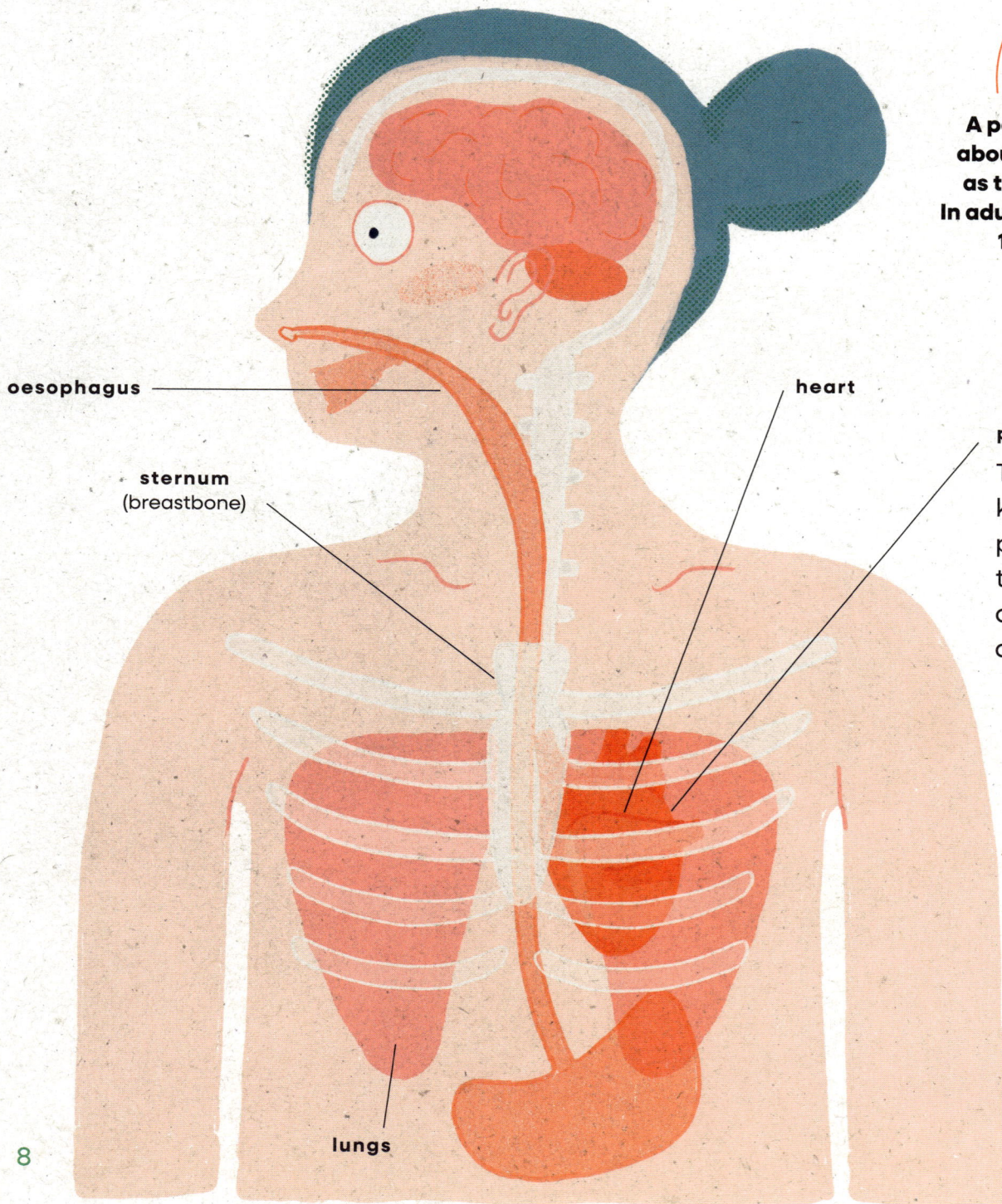

oesophagus

heart

pericardium

pericardium

The pericardium keeps the heart in place with ligaments that connect it to the diaphragm, spine and lungs.

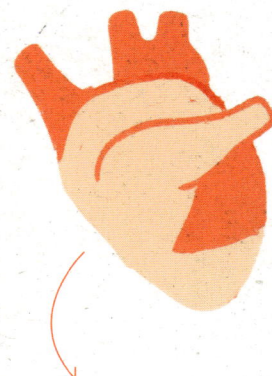

sternum
(breastbone)

The pericardium protects the heart and acts as a barrier against infection.

lungs

The weight of the heart depends on a person's age, size and weight. In adults, the heart makes up about 0.40% of a woman's weight and 0.45% of a man's weight.

Athletes have heavier hearts because they grow stronger from exercise.

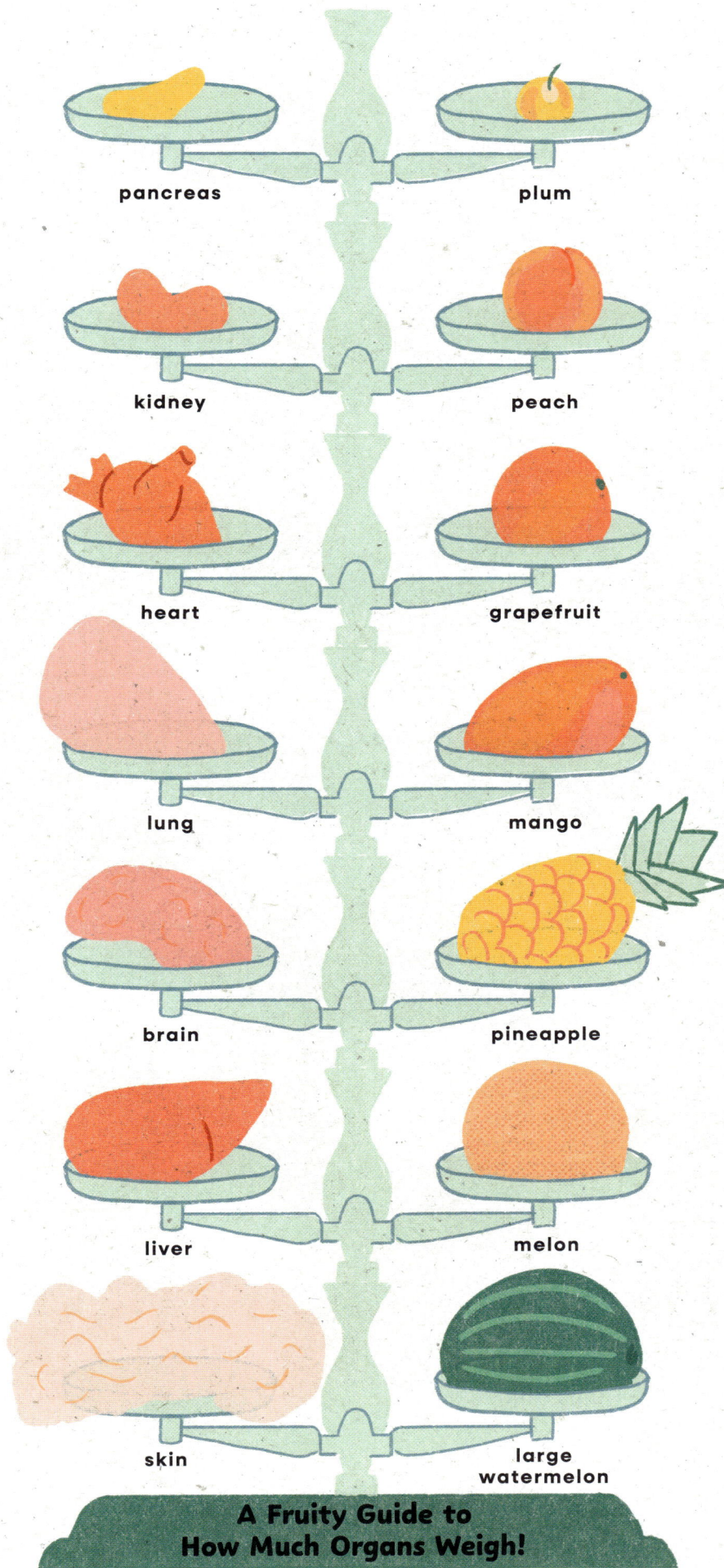

pancreas — plum

kidney — peach

heart — grapefruit

lung — mango

brain — pineapple

liver — melon

skin — large watermelon

A Fruity Guide to How Much Organs Weigh!

HOW DOES IT WORK?

The heart is a muscle that pumps blood around the body via veins and arteries. It has four chambers: two upper (the right atrium and the left atrium), and two lower (the right ventricle and the left ventricle).

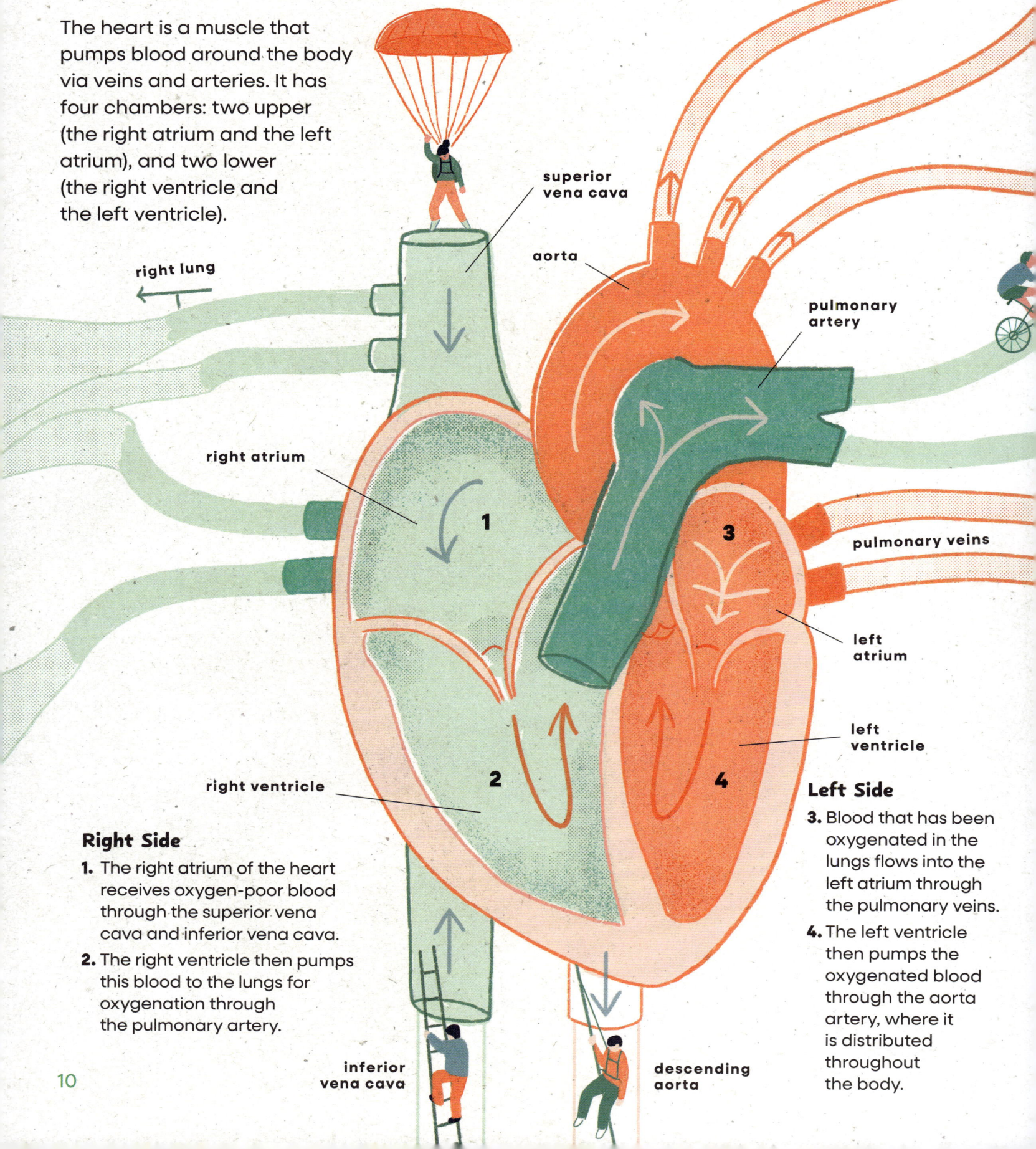

right lung

superior vena cava

aorta

pulmonary artery

right atrium

pulmonary veins

left atrium

left ventricle

right ventricle

inferior vena cava

descending aorta

Right Side

1. The right atrium of the heart receives oxygen-poor blood through the superior vena cava and inferior vena cava.

2. The right ventricle then pumps this blood to the lungs for oxygenation through the pulmonary artery.

Left Side

3. Blood that has been oxygenated in the lungs flows into the left atrium through the pulmonary veins.

4. The left ventricle then pumps the oxygenated blood through the aorta artery, where it is distributed throughout the body.

The Circulatory System

The heart receives oxygen-poor blood from the body through the veins, oxygenates it and pumps it to the rest of the body through the arteries.

left lung

The Beat of Life

With each heartbeat, blood moves through the arteries, creating a pulse. The pulse can be felt by placing fingers on the wrist or neck to count the beats. Babies can have over 150 beats per minute. At age 10, the heartbeat drops and reaches a regular rhythm of 60 to 100 beats per minute.

Important Valves

The heart valves are located at the ends of the four chambers and prevent blood from flowing backward into the heart.

Heartbeats in Action

Unlike other muscles, the heart does not need the brain to tell it to work. Instead, a special electrical system controls how fast it beats. This system is made of cells that create and send tiny signals to keep the heart pumping.

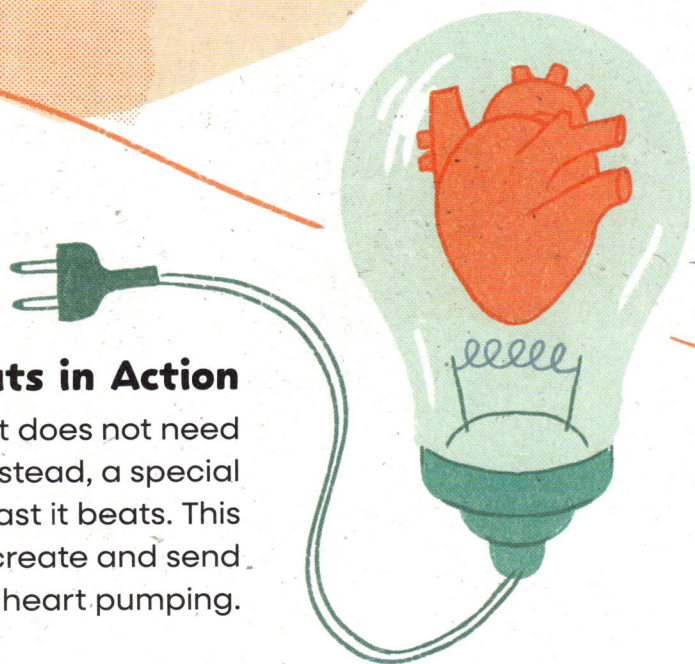

HOW HEART SCIENCE BEGAN

The oldest known case of heart disease was discovered in the mummy of an Egyptian princess from 1500 BCE.

1628

In 1628, English doctor William Harvey discovered how blood moves through the body and how the heart pumps it.

1500 BCE

2000 BCE

The Stethoscope

The stethoscope, invented by French doctor René Laënnec, is the most common tool for listening to the heart. Laënnec was shy and felt awkward putting his ear against his patients' chests. One day, he noticed a patient was uncomfortable, so he rolled a notebook into a tube to listen instead. That same day, he designed a wooden tool with two cone-shaped ends – and the first stethoscope was born!

In China, as early as 2000 BCE, people knew the heart pumped blood. In Europe, this wasn't known until the Renaissance (1300s–1600s). People once believed the heart held the soul.

In 1816, French doctor René Laënnec invented the stethoscope.

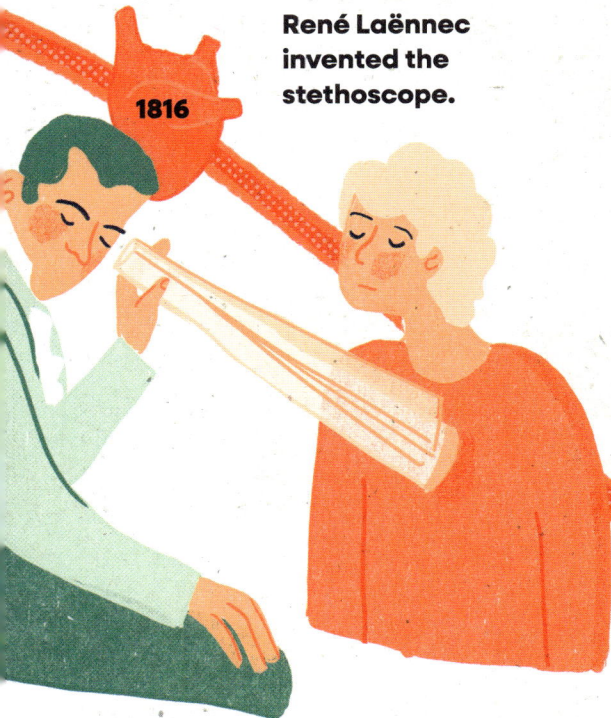

1816

In 1967, the media was captivated by an important scientific milestone: the first heart transplant in history. It was performed by Dr. Christiaan Barnard in Cape Town, South Africa.

1967

One of the first physicians to perform open heart surgery was Daniel Hale Williams in 1893. He was also the first Black heart surgeon in America.

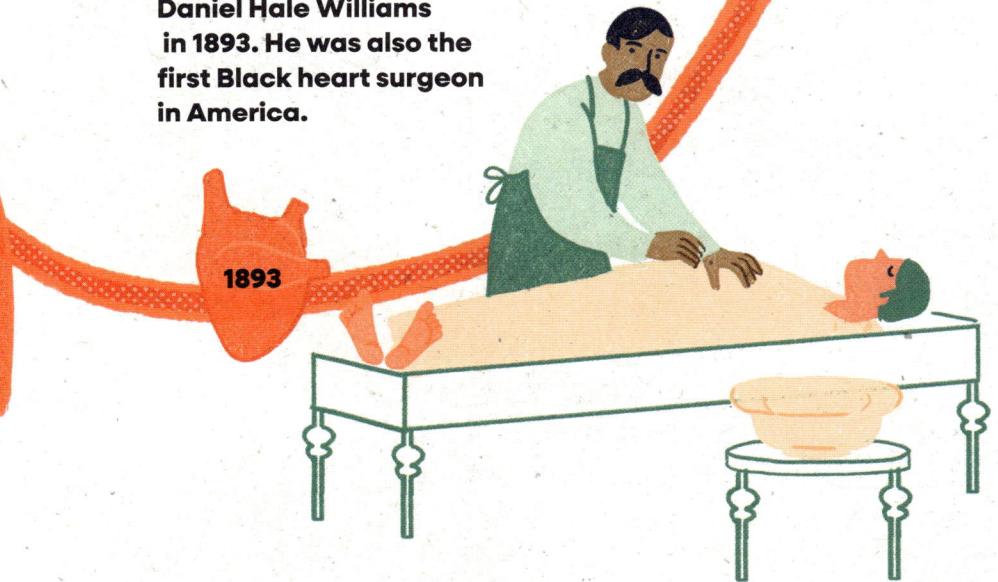

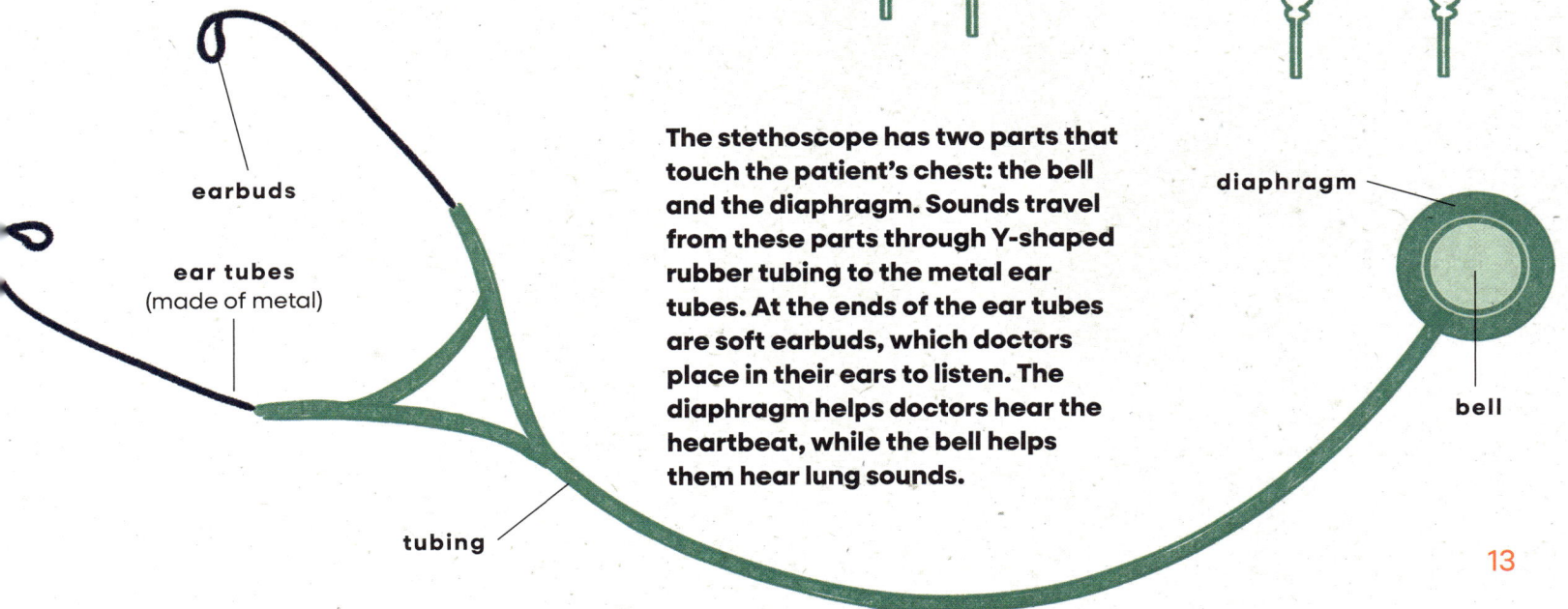

1893

earbuds

ear tubes
(made of metal)

The stethoscope has two parts that touch the patient's chest: the bell and the diaphragm. Sounds travel from these parts through Y-shaped rubber tubing to the metal ear tubes. At the ends of the ear tubes are soft earbuds, which doctors place in their ears to listen. The diaphragm helps doctors hear the heartbeat, while the bell helps them hear lung sounds.

diaphragm

bell

tubing

KEEPING YOUR HEART HAPPY

Centuries of research has helped scientists learn the best ways to keep the heart strong and healthy – and how to avoid heart problems!

Healthy Eating

In 1952, scientists Ancel and Margaret Keys discovered that countries bordering the Mediterranean Sea had very low numbers of deaths caused by heart disease. What was it about the Mediterranean diet that made it so beneficial to the heart? The answer was food rich in ingredients that reduce bad cholesterol and hypertension, which are the leading causes of cardiovascular disease.

Key Ingredients of the Mediterranean Diet

An apple a day keeps the doctor away!

fruit

olive oil

legumes and vegetables

Exercise

Physical activity, such as walking, dancing and cycling, keeps blood pressure and cholesterol levels in check.

Laughter

Laughing lowers stress levels, which can cause some cardiovascular diseases. A good laugh also boosts heart rate, respiratory rate, and oxygen consumption. Laughing for 30 minutes is as beneficial as going to the gym!

Sleep

Sleep is essential to repair and restore our body's cells and to cope with stress. Meditation, yoga, deep breathing and relaxation techniques help improve the quality of sleep.

fish

wholegrains

dried fruit

white meat

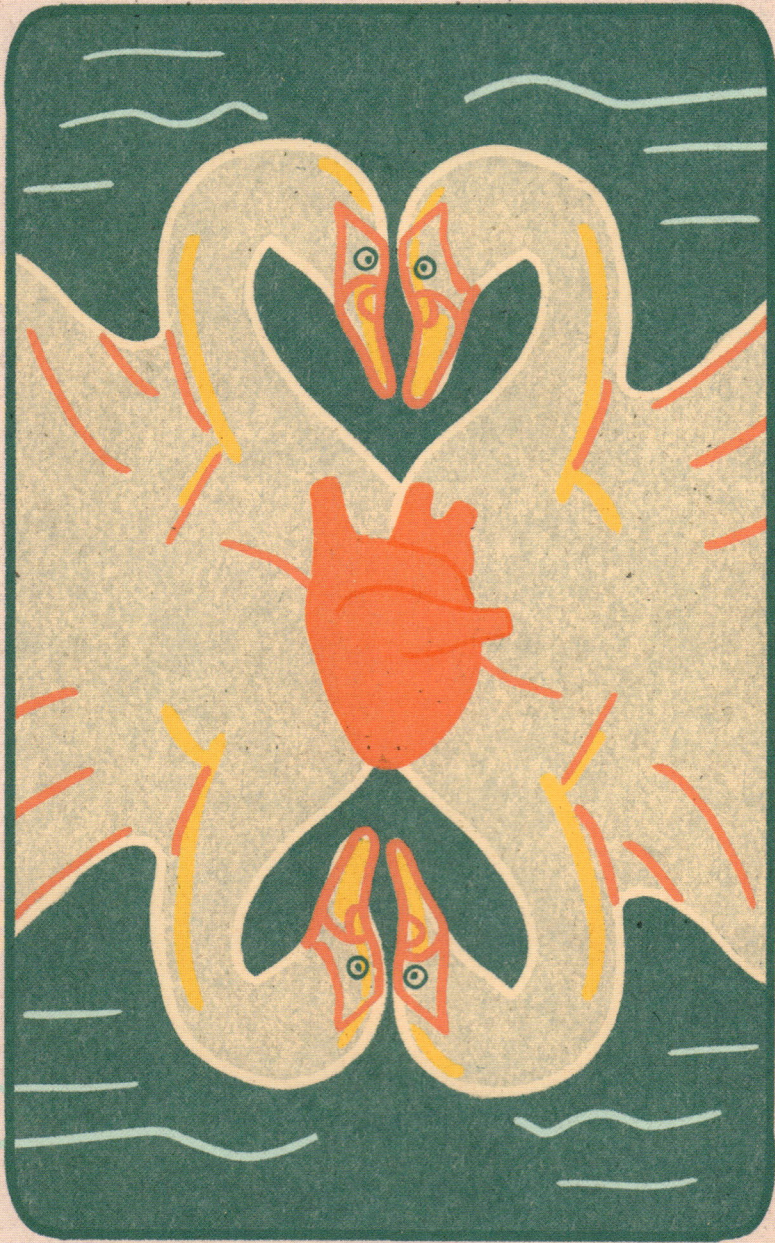

ALL ABOUT ANIMAL HEARTS

In the animal kingdom, there are many different types of hearts, from animals that have none at all to those with more than three! The heart changes in shape and size to match each species, its needs and its environment.

AMAZING ANIMAL HEARTS

Did you know some animals, like jellyfish and sponges, don't have hearts? Because they are small, slow and have simple bodies, they don't need one. Instead, they get oxygen straight from the water around them, in a process called diffusion. To move, they use body movements, like wriggling or pulsing, which allows water to flow through them. Larger animals, however, need a circulatory system with blood vessels and a heart to pump blood through their bodies. But not all hearts work the same way!

I may be heartless, but I'm not bad!

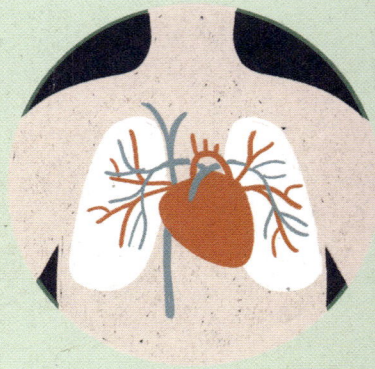

bird and mammal heart

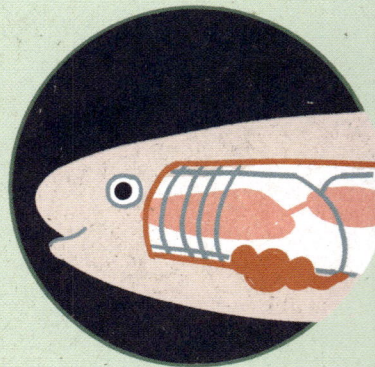

fish heart

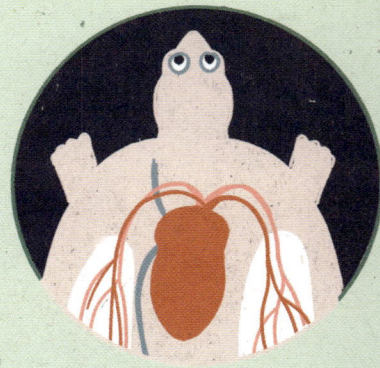

reptile heart

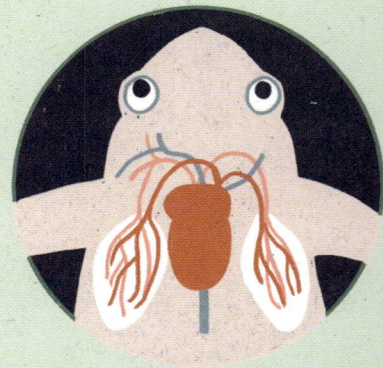

amphibian heart

Animals have two types of circulatory systems: open and closed. In an open circulatory system, blood flows freely around the organs. In a closed system, blood moves through vessels instead.

Open Circulatory System

Many invertebrates, like insects, spiders, ants and most molluscs (such as snails and clams), have an open circulatory system. Instead of flowing through blood vessels, blood-like fluid called hemolymph is pumped out of the heart and spreads over the body's tissues. When hemolymph touches the cells, it delivers nutrients and oxygen while removing waste.

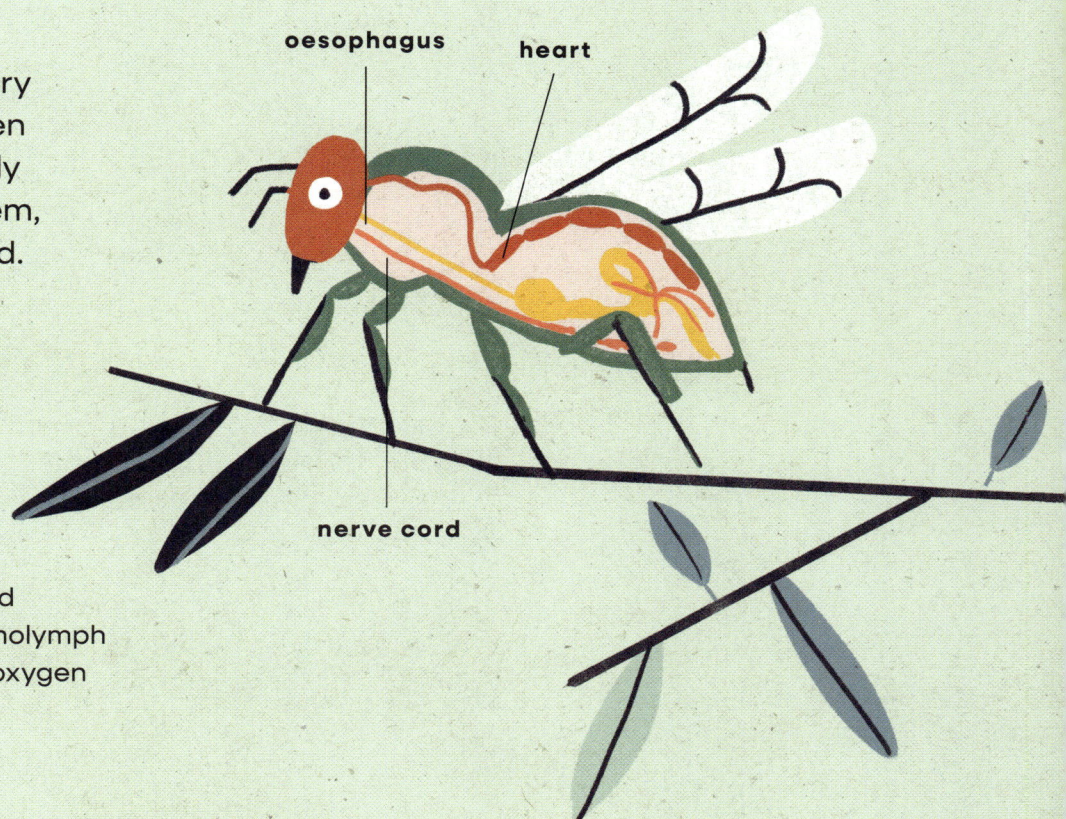

oesophagus

heart

nerve cord

Closed Circulatory System

Many vertebrates, as well as some invertebrates like worms and cephalopods (such as octopuses, squids and cuttlefish), have a closed circulatory system. Instead of flowing freely, blood stays inside vessels, moving through a continuous loop. The heart pumps blood through arteries to reach the organs, while veins carry it back to the heart.

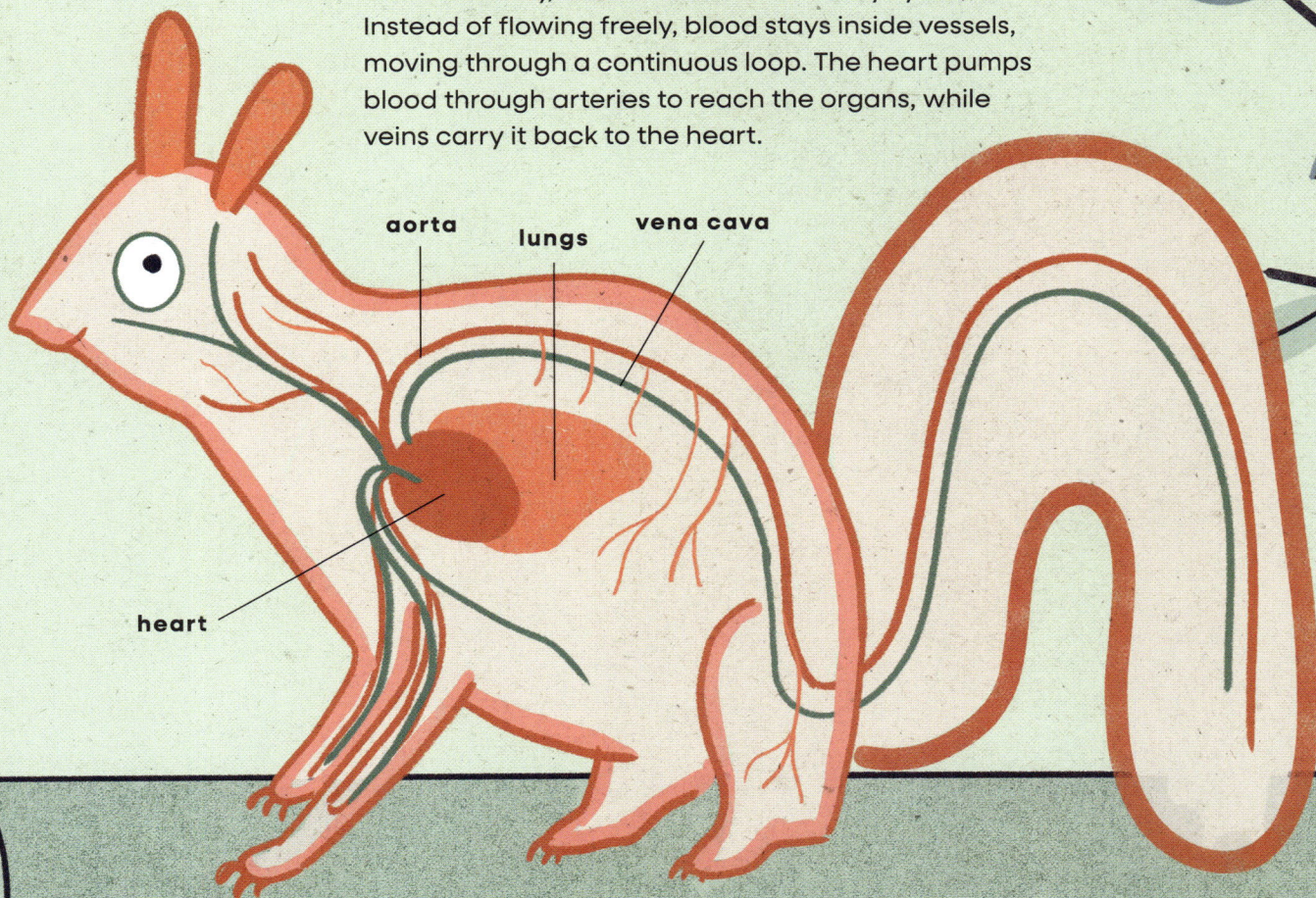

aorta

lungs

vena cava

heart

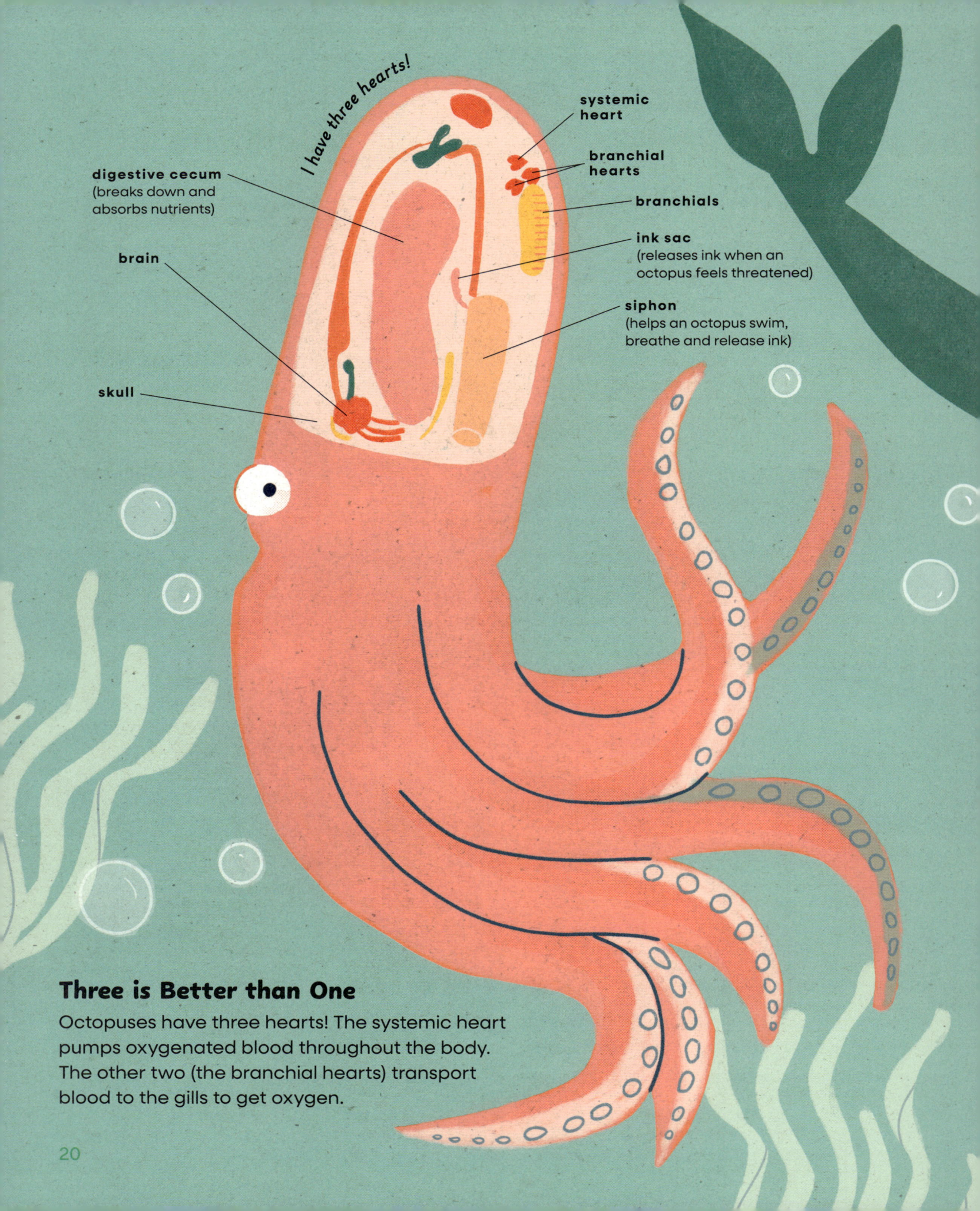

I have three hearts!

digestive cecum
(breaks down and
absorbs nutrients)

**systemic
heart**

**branchial
hearts**

branchials

ink sac
(releases ink when an
octopus feels threatened)

siphon
(helps an octopus swim,
breathe and release ink)

brain

skull

Three is Better than One

Octopuses have three hearts! The systemic heart
pumps oxygenated blood throughout the body.
The other two (the branchial hearts) transport
blood to the gills to get oxygen.

Giant Heart

In 2014, a blue whale was found off the coast of Canada. It had died after getting trapped in ice, but the cold helped to preserve its body. Scientists carefully removed its heart, which is now on display at the Royal Ontario Museum in Toronto. Weighing 180kg and measuring over a metre wide and 1.5 metres tall (about the size of a fridge), it is the largest heart ever recorded in the world!

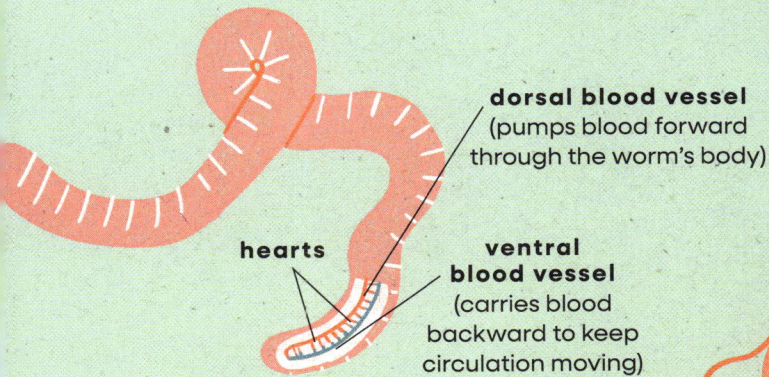

lungs

heart

dorsal blood vessel
(pumps blood forward through the worm's body)

hearts

ventral blood vessel
(carries blood backward to keep circulation moving)

A Heart Built for Heights

A giraffe's heart is uneven. Its left ventricle is much larger than the right because it needs extra strength to pump blood all the way up its long neck to the brain.

Five-Hearted Worms

Some worms have up to five hearts! They have a closed circulatory system with special blood-pumping aortic arches, which work like hearts. The number of these arches depends on the species.

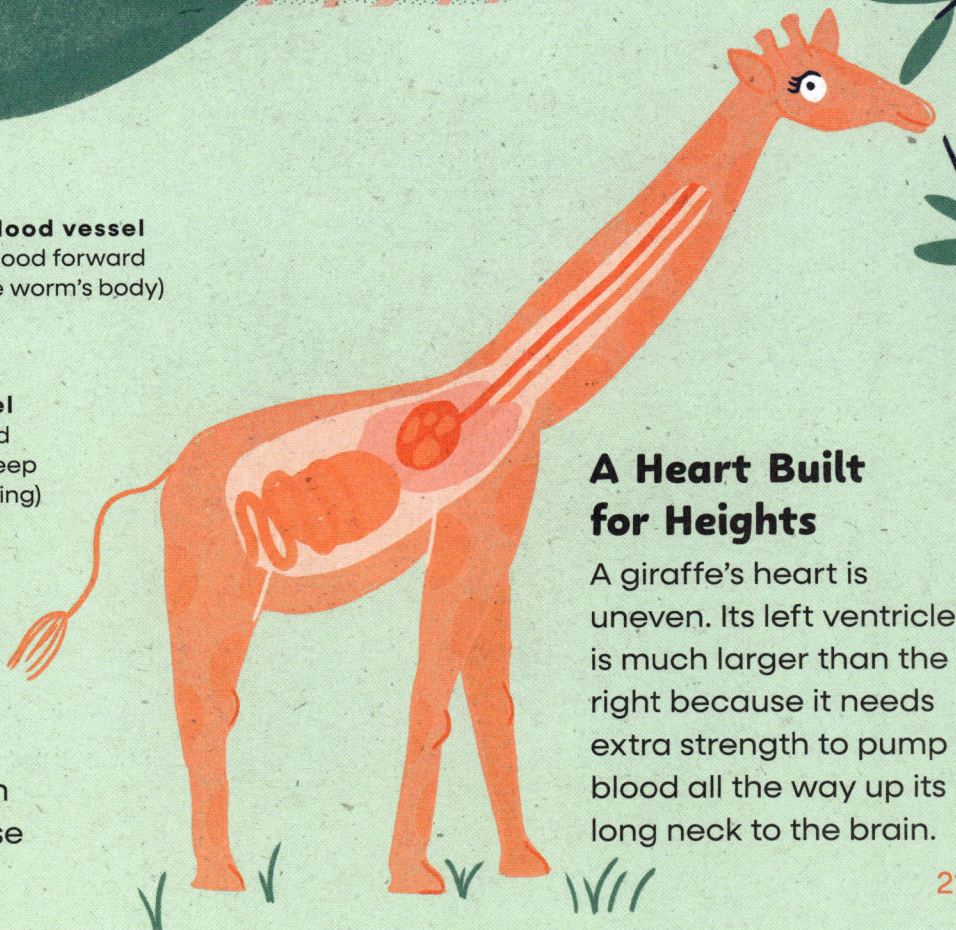

21

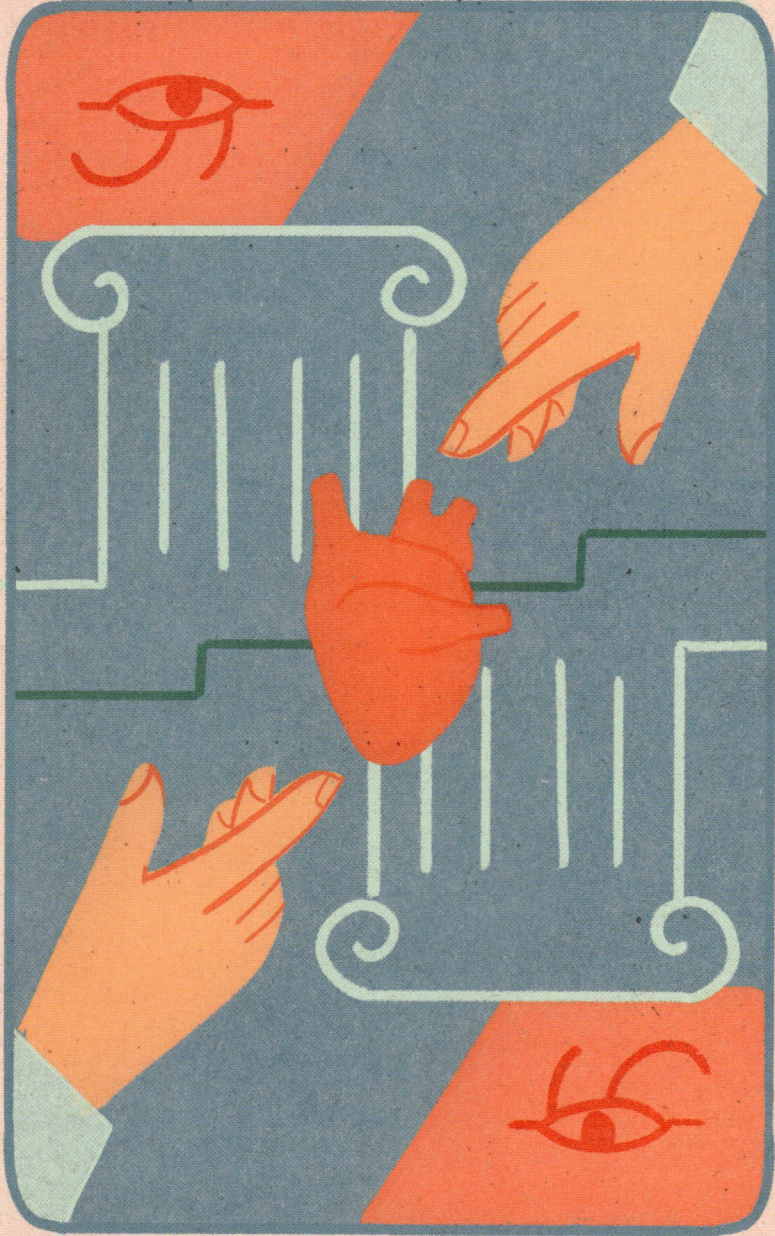

A THOUSAND AND ONE STORIES OF THE HEART

Unlike other organs in the human body, the heart is one we can feel in action. Its beats are noticeable, and the pulse changes with our emotions. Because of this, the heart has been a powerful symbol in cultures around the world throughout history.

THE HEART THROUGH HISTORY

The Egyptian Heart

In ancient Egypt, the heart was so important that there were two words for it: *ib* and *haty*. The latter referred to the physical heart, while the word *ib* referred to the consciousness – the source of thought, will, imagination, memory and life.

The Oldest Heart in Art

The earliest known drawing of a heart can be found in a Paleolithic cave painting in Asturias, Spain. The image shows a mammoth with a red spot in the centre. However, it's unclear whether the artist meant to represent a heart or if the red mark was already there before the painting.

A Heartless History

In ancient Greek and Roman culture, the liver and lungs were more important than the heart. The liver was believed to hold emotions and predict the future, while the lungs were thought to be connected to the soul.

the soul

Anubis

The heart also played a prominent role during the process of embalming mummies. While the rest of the organs were removed, the heart was embalmed using a special technique so that it would remain inside the body and could journey to the afterlife.

The ancient Egyptians believed that after death, the god Osiris judged them. Their heart was placed on a scale and weighed against a feather. If the heart was lighter, the person could live forever. But if it was too heavy, they could not enter the afterlife.

heart scarab

A heart scarab was a special beetle-shaped charm placed in tombs. People believed it could help the dead by ensuring Osiris judged their heart kindly, allowing them to enter the afterlife.

Osiris

Osiris was the powerful Egyptian god who ruled over the afterlife. He decided if the souls of the dead were worthy of eternal life.

AT THE CENTRE OF EVERYTHING

Judeo-Christian Culture

In ancient Judaism and Christianity, people believed that life came from the lungs, not the heart. In the Old and New Testaments, the heart was seen as the centre of emotions, personality and religious devotion. During the Renaissance (1300s–1600s) and Baroque (1600s–1700s) periods, focus on the heart in faith grew stronger. This led to the construction of the Basilica of the Sacred Heart in Paris, one of France's most important churches.

Aztec Heart

The Nahuatl (the language spoken by ancient Mexicans) word for 'heart' was *yóllotl*, which came from the same root as *yoli*, meaning 'to live'. This shows that these people saw the heart as the source of life itself. To them, it was the most precious gift a person could offer the gods.

Hindu Culture

Ayurveda is one of the oldest traditional medicines in the world. It teaches that the heart contains the mind and is located at the centre of the body. In the seven chakras system, Anahata is the heart chakra. It is linked to love, kindness and balance, helping people feel connected to others and themselves.

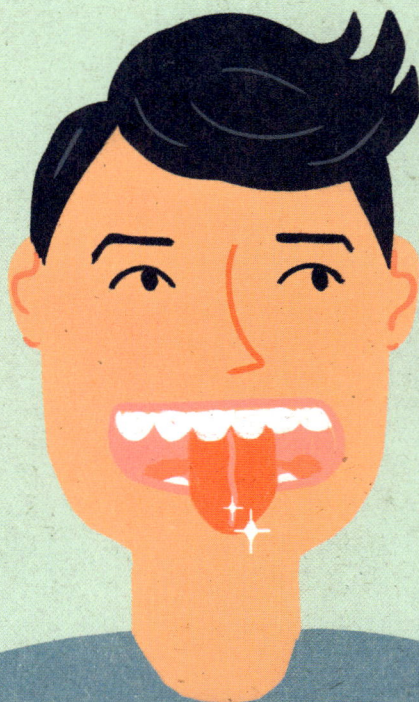

Chinese Medicine

According to Chinese tradition, the heart is an 'emperor' – leader of the body. It represents wisdom and makes good decisions with help from other organs. The heart is linked to fire, and is believed to hold the *shen*, which includes a person's thoughts, feelings, and spirit.

In Chinese tradition, the tip of the tongue reflects heart health. A light red or pink tongue means the heart is healthy, while a dark and dry tongue may show a problem, often called 'heat in the heart.'

A HEART FULL OF FEELINGS

The Sufi Heart

In Arab and Sufi traditions, spiritual love is deeply felt in the heart. This idea also appears in Andalusian poetry (from medieval Spain), which talks about love and strong emotions. Islamic poets inspired European culture and influenced the troubadours, who were poets and musicians in medieval Europe.

The Sufi dance helps people feel calm and connected to God. It starts from the heart and moves in a spinning motion. First, one hand touches the heart, then both arms open wide. Finally, one hand stays on the heart while the other reaches toward the sky. The dance shows a journey from the heart to God.

Courtly Love

From the 11th to the 15th century, a new social class called the bourgeoisie began to grow in Europe. These were educated people, like merchants and city workers, who had new ways of thinking. During this time, songs with beautiful lyrics that talked about noble and knightly love became popular. This made the heart a symbol of true love, not just an organ in the body.

ROMANTICISM

Emotions Take the Spotlight

After the Neoclassic period (when people admired Greek and Roman art) and the Enlightenment (which focused on science in the 1600s), people came to understand that emotions and imperfections were just as important as logic and order. Individual freedom (the right to think and create) was given more value. Artists started to be seen as unique creators who made art not just to please others, but for themselves and for the future.

Chopin's Heart

The composer and pianist Frédéric Chopin was one of the Romantic artists. He had tuberculosis (a lung disease) and was very afraid of being buried alive. Before he died, he asked his sister, Ludwika, to take his heart after his death. She fulfilled his wish – she secretly sent his heart back to Poland, his home country, while his body was buried in Paris.

The musician's heart was kept safe in the Church of the Holy Cross in Warsaw. But during the Second World War, the church was bombed and destroyed. According to legend, a Nazi officer who admired Chopin saved the heart. It was finally returned to the rebuilt church by a Polish cardinal, where it remains today.

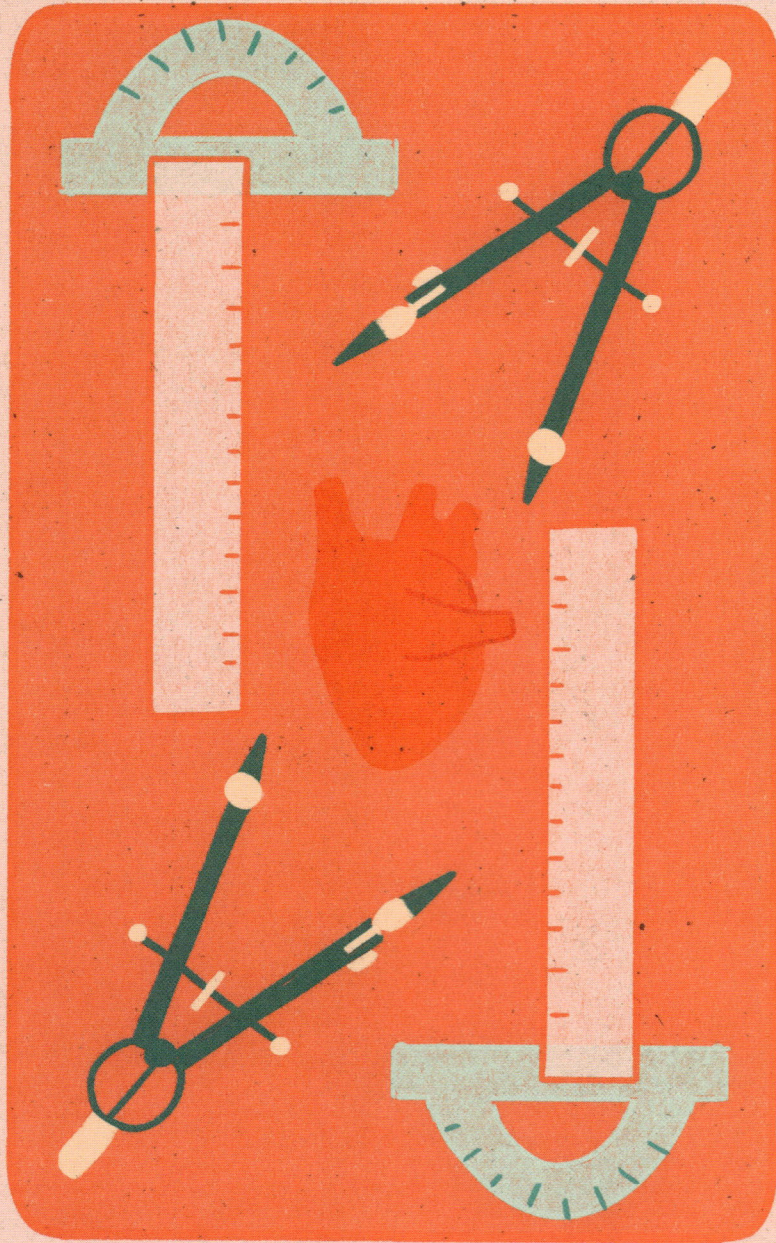

THE SHAPE OF THE HEART

The heart symbol, with its two rounded arches meeting at a point in the shape of a 'V,' is the most famous sign of love and romantic emotions. This shape has been used since ancient times and has become a universal symbol recognised all over the world!

A SYMBOL OF LOVE

Etruscan Culture

Ivy is a plant that, in Etruscan culture (an ancient Italian civilisation), was considered a symbol of immortality and rebirth because it is evergreen. It is also a climbing plant that clings to itself and its surroundings. For this reason, ivy became a symbol of loyalty and friendship.

ivy

Ancient Greece

In Ancient Greece, brides and grooms were crowned with wreaths of ivy during wedding ceremonies. People also used ivy to decorate pottery. It was meant to represent nature, but it just so happens that its leaves look a lot like little hearts.

Silphium

The famous Roman writer, Pliny the Elder, once wrote of a plant found in Greece that is now extinct. Called silphium, it was of great importance in both cooking and medicine.

silphium

silphium seed

Silphium was so highly valued that the coins of the Greek colony of Cyrene (in present-day Libya) were engraved with a heart shape to represent the silphium seed.

BE MY VALENTINE

The heart became more popular as a symbol of love during the Victorian Era when people exchanged cards on Valentine's Day. The idea came from old images of courtly love, a type of romance in the Middle Ages where knights showed their admiration for noble ladies. By the 1900s, these cards were produced in large numbers, making the heart symbol even more famous.

My arrow of gold is the one you wish for!

Cupid's Magic Arrows

Cupid often appeared on Valentine's Day cards exchanged by sweethearts. According to Greek mythology, Cupid is Eros, the god of love, and the son of Venus (the goddess of love) and Mars (the god of war). He carries two special arrows – a golden one with dove feathers that makes people fall in love, and a lead one with owl feathers, which causes hatred or indifference.

Saint Valentine of Rome

Valentine's Day has Catholic origins. At a time when Christianity was forbidden, a priest called Valentine of Rome secretly married soldiers to their fiancées, even though it was considered a crime at the time. The emperor (Claudius II) had forbidden soldiers to marry as he thought this would make them better fighters. Once discovered, Claudius imprisoned Valentine and condemned him to death. According to legend, while in prison, Valentine learned that the daughter of the judge was blind, so he prayed to God to restore her sight. He also wrote her a note and gave it to her before he was beheaded on February 14, 270 BCE (now remembered as Valentine's Day). She did not understand why he had written to her if he knew she was blind, but miraculously, she was able to read the words on the paper: 'From your Valentine.'

HISTORY'S GREATEST LOVE STORIES

Stronger Than Politics

Cleopatra, queen of ancient Egypt, lost her throne and returned to take back her power. She fell in love with Mark Antony, a Roman general who ruled Rome with two others. Cleopatra and Mark Antony's political alliance lasted 14 years. But their story ended in tragedy. Mark Antony was told Cleopatra had died – but it was false! Heartbroken, he took his own life. Cleopatra knew she would be captured and humiliated in Rome, so she let a poisonous snake bite her, choosing to die with her lover than accept her fate. Their love story shook the Roman Empire.

Forbidden Love

Another famous love story is set in China. At the age of 19, a young man called Liu fell in love with a widowed woman, Xu, who was 10 years his senior and the mother of two children. Faced with the rejection of their families and society, the couple went to live in a cave in the mountains, far from everything. It is said that Liu built his wife a staircase of over 6,000 steps so that she could go down to visit the village. It is known today as the staircase of love.

Love in a Hopeless Place

Nadine Hwang was the daughter of a Chinese diplomat, and Nelly Mousset-Vos was a Belgian opera singer. During the Second World War, they were both sent to Ravensbrück, a dangerous prison camp in Germany. There, they met and fell in love. Later, Nelly was sent to another camp, but she miraculously managed to survive. Nadine also escaped and reached Sweden, a safe country. After the war ended, they found each other again and were reunited.

THE HEART IN POPULAR CULTURE

Free Love

In the 1970s, the hippie movement was popular. Hippies were people who believed in peace, love and freedom. During this time, the heart symbol was officially recognised as a symbol of universal love.

The Digital Heart

In today's digital era, the heart continues to be popular. It's often used to symbolise life in video games, and is a symbol of affinity and appreciation on social media.

We see hearts everywhere!

sunglasses

The Queen of Hearts

Q

emoticons

tattoos

MAMA

coffee

lollipops

Pop Culture Icon

In the 1980s, the artist Keith Haring popularised the heart symbol through his paintings. It was also prominently featured by famous artists such as Damien Hirst and Jeff Koons, who created bold, eye-catching art inspired by kitsch – a style that is often playful, colourful and exaggerated.

We can even make a heart symbol with our hands!

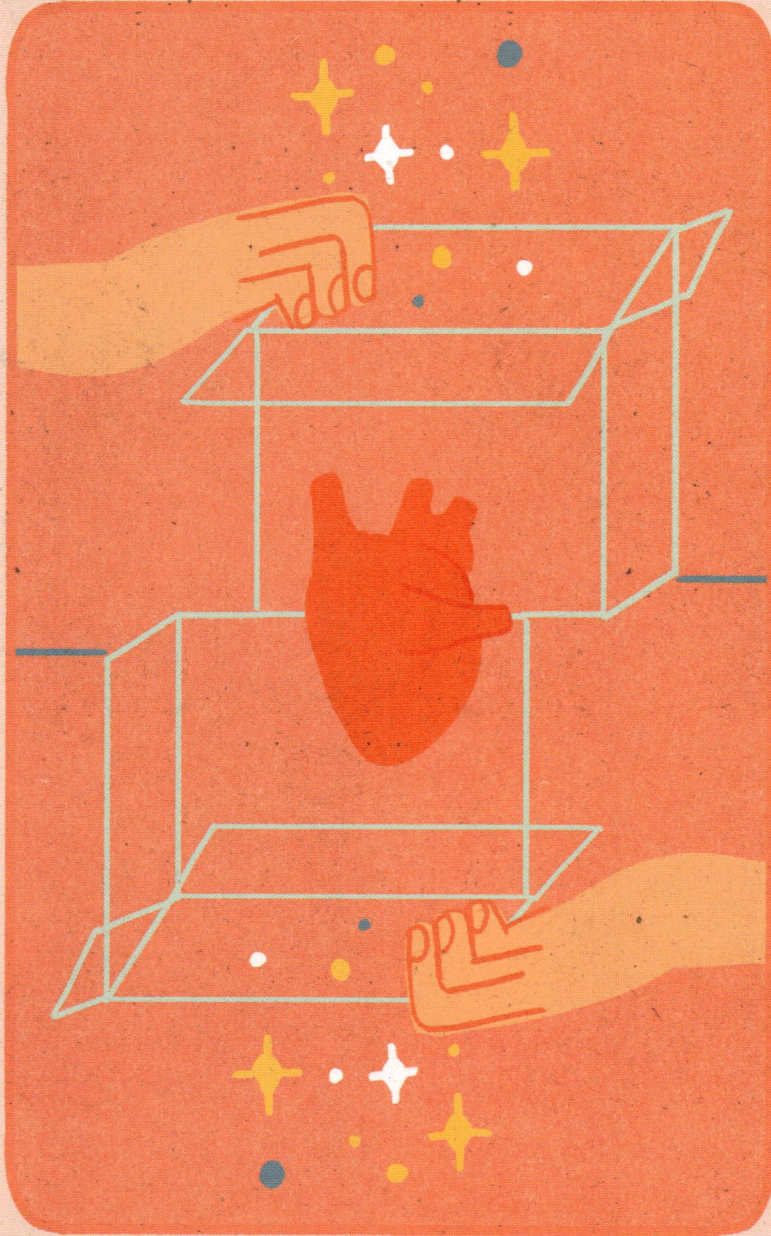

SPEAKING FROM THE HEART

The heart is so special that people have used it in metaphors – a way of comparing things – in many languages. For example, when we say that someone is 'hard-hearted', we picture someone who is cold and unfeeling.

TELLING THE TRUTH

The heart is often used to represent true feelings – especially emotions that we don't always show. That is why many languages have expressions like 'to speak from the heart' which means to speak honestly, or 'to wear your heart on your sleeve', which means to show your emotions.

English ·················· *To speak from the heart*

Spanish ·················· *Hablar desde el corazón*

Italian ·················· *Parlare col cuore*

French ·················· *Parler du fond du cœur*

German ·················· *Aus dem Herz sprechen*

The Heart's Thermometer

The temperature of the heart can often signify feelings too. For example, to be 'cold-hearted' means to be insensitive, to have no feelings. And, 'to have your heart on fire' means to feel intense love and passion.

You have a cold heart.

My heart is telling me...

How the Heart Speaks to Us

The heart also has the capacity to 'speak' to us. When we say that the heart is 'telling us something', we are referring to our intuition, meaning we have a feeling about something or someone.

What is the Heart Made Of?

What the heart is 'made' of can also be used to indicate what we think of other people. For example, if someone has a heart 'made of gold' it means they are a good person. However, if someone has a heart 'of stone', it means they have no sympathy or interest in others.

Measuring Kindness

The size of the heart has connotations too. In many languages, a big heart is synonymous with generosity or goodness. It suggests that the heart can carry emotions, and the larger it is, the more feelings it can hold. On the other hand, absence of the heart is perceived as being evil, ruthless or hard-hearted.

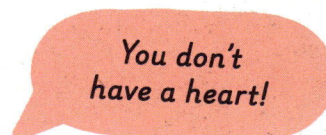

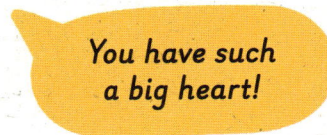

You have such a big heart!

You don't have a heart!

BROKEN HEARTS AND PLATONIC LOVE

The heart as a symbol of love appears in a text that is over 4,000 years old. The poem, *The Epic of Gilgamesh*, written in the ancient language of Akkadian, is the first of humankind's great literary epics. But the metaphor of the broken heart is represented in many languages too . . .

To have a broken heart — English

Tener el corazón roto — Spanish

Avere il cuore spezzato — Italian

Avoir le coeur brisé — French

Ein gebrochenes Herz haben — German

In literature, love that is symbolised as a heart is considered precious, delicate, fragile, and susceptible to being broken.

HISTORY'S BROKEN HEARTS

An Impossible Love

Dante Alighieri was an Italian writer from the Middle Ages. When he was nine years old, he met Beatrice Portinari, who was eight at the time. Even though she later married someone else and sadly died very young, Dante never stopped loving her. She became his muse (a person who inspires art) and he made her the main character in his famous poem, the *Divine Comedy*.

A Painful Love

Frida Kahlo and Diego Rivera were two famous artists from Mexico. They were married, but their relationship was difficult. Diego often had other girlfriends, and Frida knew. She accepted this, but when she found out that Diego had been in a relationship with her own sister, she was very upset. She took revenge by starting a relationship with Leon Trotsky, a Russian politician who Diego admired. This caused big problems in their marriage, and they got divorced. However, one year later, they remarried.

A Love in the Shadows

Designer Jed Johnson met artist Andy Warhol when he began working at the artist's studio: The Factory. There, they fell in love and started a relationship that lasted for 12 years. But Warhol was unfaithful and was often absent from the house where they lived. Johnson, who felt he lived in Warhol's shadow, wanted to establish himself as an independent artist and designer. This caused them to have many disagreements.

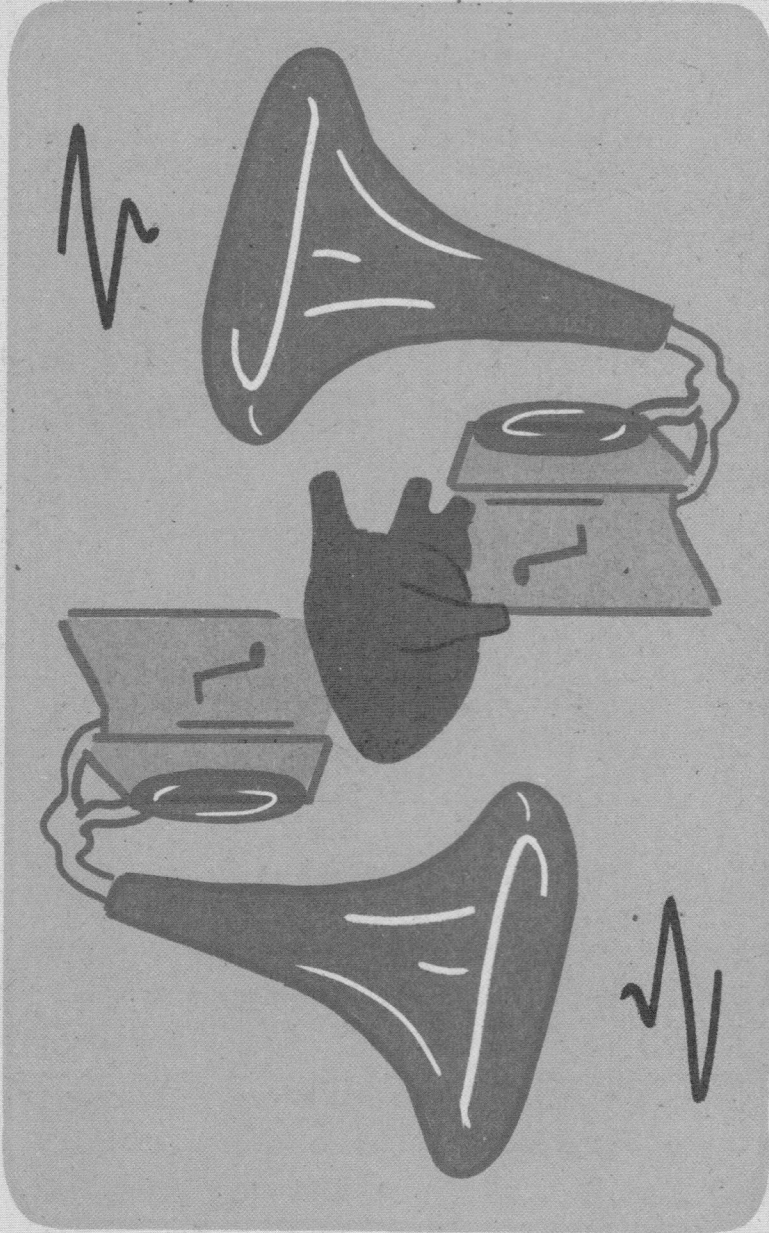

THE PULSE OF LIFE

Boom boom, boom boom, boom boom. If you cover your ears, you can hear your heartbeat. It's the sound inside you. We have heard this sound since we were in our mother's wombs, and it is like music that accompanies us wherever we go.

THE PULSE OF LIFE

The Beat as a Measure of Time

John Cage was a musician from the 20th century who liked to create unusual music. He wanted to experience absolute silence. To test this, he locked himself in a special room at Harvard University, called an anechoic chamber. The room blocked all outside sounds. But even in that quiet room, he could still hear the noise of his breathing and the beating of his heart. He realised that true silence doesn't exist!

In music, the pulse is like its heartbeat. It is the steady beat that keeps the music moving. Other parts of music, like melody, harmony and rhythm, are added on top of this beat.

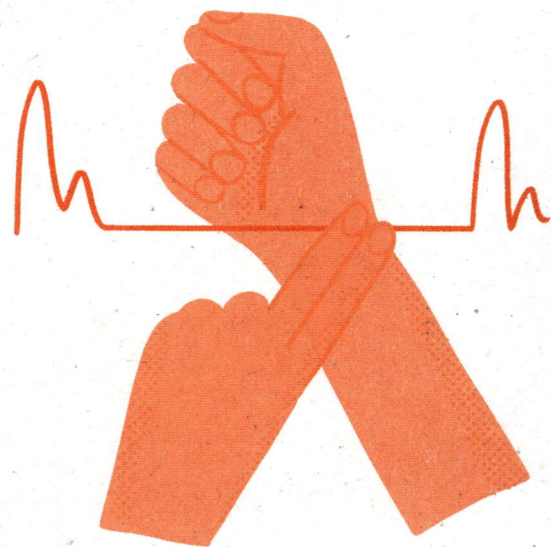

In dance music the pulse is usually fast . . .

How Does Music Affect the Heartbeat?

Studies show that our heartbeat can change with music. When we listen to fast music, our heart rate increases and our breathing quickens. But when the music is slow, our hearts beat slower and we feel calmer.

time scale

pendulum

weight of pendulum

box

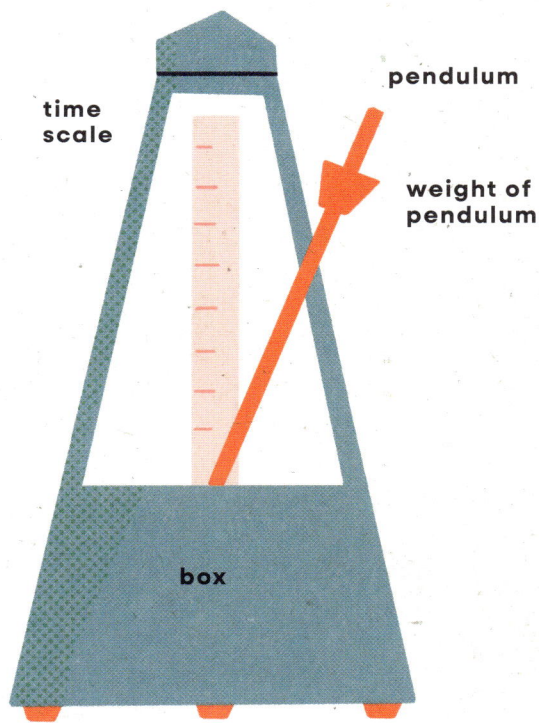

The Metronome

Invented in the early 1800s, the metronome is a device used to measure the tempo, or the speed, of a piece of music. The tempo is measured in beats per minute (bpm), which is the number of times the metronome beats in one minute. Before the metronome was invented, musicians used words to define the speed of music, such as the Italian terms *allegro*, *vivace*, *andante* or *presto*. *Vivace* corresponds to a tempo of between 126 and 144 beats per minute and also indicates that the music should be played with a lively tone.

. . . and in lullabies the pulse is always slow.

44–50 BPM

50–60 BPM

60–80 BPM

80–100 BPM

LARGO/LARGHETTO (very slow)

LENTO/ADAGIO (slow and relaxed)

ANDANTE/ANDANTINO (walking pace)

MODERATO (moderate speed)

100–126 BPM

126–144 BPM

144–208 BPM

ALLEGRETTO/ ALLEGRO (fairly fast/fast and lively)

VIVACE (lively and quick)

PRESTO/PRESTISSIMO (very fast)

47

Published in the UK in 2026 by Post Wave Children's Books,
an imprint of Post Wave Publishing UK Ltd,
Runway East, 24-28 Bloomsbury Way, London, WC1A 2SN

www.postwavepublishing.com

A catalogue record of this book is available from the British Library.

First edition 2024, published with permission of Zahorí Books
Original title: *Un cor: història, ciència i molt d'amor*
Text and illustration copyright © 2024 by Noemí Fabra
Design copyright © 2024 by Joana Casals at Zahorí Books
English translation copyright © 2025 by Gabriella Aldeman

Copyright © Zahorí Books, Spain, 2024

10 9 8 7 6 5 4 3 2 1
0825 002

ISBN 978-1-83627-091-1

Printed and manufactured in China
by Leo Paper Products in Heshan, Guangdong

This book conforms to General Product Safety
Regulation (GPSR) requirements.
EU authorised representative: Harriet Birkinshaw,
Post Wave Berlin Studio
Email: GPSR@postwavepublishing.com
Address: Post Wave Berlin Studio,
c/o Mindspace, Skalitzer Straße 104,
10997 Berlin, Germany

FSC
www.fsc.org
MIX
Paper | Supporting
responsible forestry
FSC® C020056